Parenting

How to Deal with Misbehaving and Challenging Toddlers

B. Thompson

Introduction

I want to thank you and congratulate you for downloading the book, "Parenting-How to Deal with Misbehaving and Challenging Toddlers".

This book contains proven steps and strategies on how to tame your toddlers especially when their behavior becomes out of hand. As children move from being babies to toddlers, they are amazed at the unbelievable freedom that appears right before their very eyes. Suddenly, they can stand, walk, eat, explore, and run on their own. They have the ability to think on their own, touch, feel, manipulate objects and a whole lot of crazy things a parent could dare imagine.

This book is created with parents of toddlers in mind. There is no more important responsibility in life than that of being a parent. Parenting is a full-time job, regardless if you have an outside, corporate career or not. You may take time off from your job, but you are never off the clock when it comes to being a parent.

In this book, you will learn how to tame, discipline, and deal with challenging toddlers, understand their behavior and what needs to be done when they are becoming uncontrollable, and other techniques to help discipline this interesting little person.

Thanks again for downloading this book, I hope you enjoy it!

© Copyright 2014 by
_____ - All rights reserved.

This document is geared towards providing exact and reliable information in regards to the topic and issue covered. The publication is sold with the idea that the publisher is not required to render accounting, officially permitted, or otherwise, qualified services. If advice is necessary, legal or professional, a practiced individual in the profession should be ordered.

- From a Declaration of Principles which was accepted and approved equally by a Committee of the American Bar Association and a Committee of Publishers and Associations.

In no way is it legal to reproduce, duplicate, or transmit any part of this document in either electronic means or in printed format. Recording of this publication is strictly prohibited and any storage of this document is not allowed unless with written permission from the publisher. All rights reserved.

The information provided herein is stated to be truthful and consistent, in that any liability, in terms of inattention or otherwise, by any usage or abuse of any policies, processes, or directions contained within is the solitary and utter responsibility of the recipient reader. Under no circumstances will any legal responsibility or blame be held against the publisher for any reparation, damages, or monetary loss due to the information herein, either directly or indirectly.

Respective authors own all copyrights not held by the publisher.

The information herein is offered for informational purposes solely, and is universal as so. The presentation of the information is without contract or any type of guarantee assurance.

The trademarks that are used are without any consent, and the publication of the trademark is without permission or backing by the trademark owner. All trademarks and brands within this book are for clarifying purposes only and are the owned by the owners themselves, not affiliated with this document.

Chapter 1 – The Toddler – A Curious Little Person

In the case of behavioral development, we can expect our children to go through four different stages in the early years of their lives. The first stage is from birth until your child reaches 1 year old. This is primarily called the baby stage.

Stage 2 goes from 1 to 2 ½ years old called the younger toddler. Stage 3 is from 2 ½ to 4 years old known as the preschool toddler. Finally, stage 4 from 4 years old up to 8 years of age or called the early school-age child. Within this said framework, children grow in size and behavior. Their behavior will change, but not necessarily for the better. This is where parents like you come in.

For toddlers, having the ability to finally do things on their own given their acceleration of freedom, this stage is exciting. For parents, toddlerhood is the perfect time to teach their kids early on of controls and limits. This will be all about learning to control their bodies and behavior.

Some of the following controls include:

- Control of behavior – learning that tantrums are not the right way to get parents' attention and influence them

- Control of bodily functions – such as being toilet or potty trained

- Control over selfishness – learning that toys and food are meant to be shared. Even attention from parents and everything that he thinks belongs to him are to be shared.

- Control over frustration – it is like knowing and understanding that their so called "freedom" does not always mean they can do things successfully. Perfect examples are feeding, bathing, and changing clothes.

- Control of separation anxiety – moving from close clinginess to be on their own at preschool, and later on, big school.

What Makes Toddlers Tick

Whether you think they are heaven sent, big treasure, terrible 2-year-old, or an explorer, all toddlers have one thing in common. They have these behavioral traits you never dared imagine existed. Some of these traits include:

Toddlers have little to zero sense

Ages 1 to 2 years old, toddlers are considered to have zero sense. It is because, during this time, all they got is maximum mobility and minimum sense. We all know that this combination is psychologically upsetting for parents like you. This is the stage wherein your toddler is unthinking and will just do what he pleases – climbing up and down staircases, scattering toys, eating inedible stuff, and a whole lot more.

Toddlers at this age also get into trouble fighting with their siblings, and they do not know when to stop. Other unthinking behaviors include head-banging, spilling milk on bed sheets, and just simply messing around the whole house. For effective discipline, parents should know when it is best to just slow down or admit defeat. Unfortunately, for some, admitting defeat is impossible thinking that they should be the one in control and in command. While this is true, there will be instances when it is better off to just rest your case.

What is even more frustrating is that there are parents who are making heavy weather of bringing up their children. They often misunderstand these behaviors that they thought their children exist only to annoy them. They slowly forget the fun of having kids around and begin to focus on parenting as an exhausting task and routine.

Toddlers are self-centered

This is a fact; toddlers only focus on their own happiness and needs. They do not have a care in the world simply because they are still young and do not understand what is going on. It is like having a tunnel vision where all they see and care is for their own best and interest.

Sharing of toys or politely asking for it is never going to happen if you have a toddler around. The idea of taking turns is quite foreign at this age as well. And although they love being around other children, they are more focused on being beside kids their age rather than being with them.

For parents, you don't have to worry, this behavior is normal. As the years progress and as your toddler matures, he will surely get through self-centeredness.

Toddlers want constant attention from parents

Most of the time, toddlers love to be the center of attention. If you notice, when your toddler is with another toddler or with a number of kids, the one who steals the limelight will surely be hated. This example does not only extend to playmates but even to simple chores and activities such as cooking, a lengthy phone call, or even when their daddy suddenly hugs or kisses mommy.

Attention is important to toddlers. Since they have little to zero sense, all they think and believe is that mommy or daddy is always there for them. But after a day of messy play, trying to keep the house in order in between plays, and taking care of your toddler's needs, parents are already exhausted. What's more is that you are not just going to do it for 24 hours, but for the rest of your life or as long as they need a Mom and Dad beside them.

The "No" word

Think how many times you have said this word to your toddler. According to experts, toddlers only copy what they hear and see from their parents, and learn to say the word "no" long before they learn to say "yes'.

Toddlers have short attention span

Have a toddler sit on a chair with a toy or food on his hand, and he will last doing the activity only for 3 – 5 minutes. 3 minutes if he finds it interesting and 5 minutes if he begins to be more curious about it. What does this mean? It means that they only live for the here and now. Therefore, it is at this age when constant supervision, guidance, and praises come into play.

And so, if you have a toddler who whines all the time, who demands more stage position, who is self-centered, and has more power than sense, do not fret. You are not the only parent who is going through or has gone through the same situation. Parents, these are all normal behaviors, so there is no need for blaming or for feeling unworthy or not good enough for your children. Just be the best Mom and Dad that you can be, and go with the flow. Who knows, you might learn a thing or two with your terrible 2's.

Chapter 2 – Parenting 101 – On Disciplining Techniques

There must be confidence in parenting. Confidence is what makes parents positive, in charge, and effective. Notice that when your confidence level is high, the daily hassles of living and dealing with challenging toddlers become an easy feat. But when your confidence crumbles, just like parents experience most of the time, you will quickly lose all the right perspective that you have set and that easy feat, walk in the park day suddenly becomes one messy and extra exhausting day.

Confidence has an effect in everything that you do. For parents, confidence brings forth effective discipline, which ultimately improves your child's behavior and builds his own self-confidence as well. But just how confident are you in parenting your children? Are you the type who is 50-50? Are you unsure if what you are doing is right? It may be a bit strange that despite self-help books, how-to manuals, and child care professionals, parents still feel short when it comes to parenting. You need to appear sure in your decisions even if you are not. If you've ever been travelling and a car and two people tell you different directions. Who is the one you usually go with? The majority of the time it's the person who is most sure in what they are saying. This is a certainty bias which means we are more likely to believe and follow people who are certain in what they are doing. Your child needs to know that you know what you are doing. They are reliant on you, so make sure you back up your decisions with confidence.

Yes, life has become tough for parents today because of many different factors such as becoming overwhelmed with information, isolation, lifestyle, competition, and many more. What is important is that you are confident that you are doing a great job, although most parents fail to realize this. The fact that you are lovingly attending to your toddler's every need, waking up in the middle of the night to change his nappies or feed him – these are all good reasons to worry about how you parent your child.

Remember, parenting is a compromise. We start with high ideals but later on lower the sights simply because you are human, and you become tired and exhausted. It is not for you to compare. What feels right and works for you is as good a way to bring up your children as any other parents do. Just keep in mind that if you love your kids, you must enjoy them. Do what feels right and learn to slow down. Not soon enough, you will find yourselves with kids no longer expressing the needs to have their parents around. So for as long as they need you, be there, and give the best you've got.

How to Discipline A Child in A Way That doesn't Affect Their Self Esteem Later in Life

What we say to our kids has a profound effect on their self-image. Words that come out when we're in a highly emotional state could define their lives. Children grow up thinking they're bad and attach their identity to be that person, and it leads to a whole road of trouble. What we say can have a massive effect on the child's self-esteem. We want our children to have every advantage they can in life and it's our responsibility to help ensure this. According to leading self-esteem expert Nathaniel Branden the best way to punish a child for a wrong they have committed is the following: Condemn the action and not the child. This means tell the child, what they have done is bad instead of, the child themselves being bad. By doing this, you teach the child a sense of morality without causing them to form an identity to a specific action. Think about it, you are their main authority in life. You teach them the majority of the things they know, if you tell them that they are bad, enough times at an impressionable age, they'll start to believe you and develop an identity around it. It can be a major hindrance to self-esteem which is something everyone deserves. So condemn the action and not the child.

Techniques of Discipline

If there is one thing parents need to know when it comes to parenting, it is the fact that is not all about punishment. Discipline is about encouraging, shaping, and rewarding your toddler to behave in the correct way. Discipline should be something positive rather than the nasty, negative stuff.

So what is the best way?

First, you need to start with the tone of voice. A parent should learn how to say encouraging words such as "Good job", "You did well", "You are so good", Well done" – all these coupled with the way you look at your toddler when you say it and how you hold him will all make a big difference. What is important is that you learn how to transmit that love through your eyes and words. Think about this, one of the main goals for your toddler is to get your attention. If they get more attention by misbehaving than doing something good, they'll misbehave. It wouldn't make sense for them to go for the option that provides less attention. So really play up the fact when they do something good.

These kinds of tones and actions should be mainly used in disciplining your toddler. When they are not behaving the way you would want them to be, you again transmit your message with your voice, only this time firmer, more serious, and with a tone of disapproval. You don't have to shout just to send your message across. If you are shouting, they will realize it's a more effective way to get your attention. They may not understand the whole thing, but at least they know that you are not pleased with the behavior.

The following are tips on how to discipline your challenging toddler without resorting to that old smacking or "go to your room" method.

1. Know what winds up your toddler – you probably know by now what makes your child misbehave and what makes them and the rest of the household have a terrible day. Knowing the trigger before it becomes a full blown, hard to control one. The best confrontation is one that doesn't happen. If it can be prevented. Sometimes it will necessary to show your child if something is or isn't acceptable however other times it can be avoided if you know what sets them off.

   Take, for example, bringing your child to supermarkets or in the cinemas. Some parents would question why their toddler misbehaves at these places while other children do not. What they do not know is that there are those parents who never really bring their children to supermarkets and cinemas because they will know what will happen and they know exactly how their children would behave in such places. And so, they intentionally avoid these places. So if you know that bringing your toddler to a supermarket will only make them throw tantrums, and you can avoid bringing them, do not bring them. It is as simple as that. You should also keep in mind it is best to take your toddler shopping at a time when they are not tired. It can be a big emotional drain on them doing this, so try to take them at a time where they are alert to decrease the chances of a tantrum.

2. They want your undivided attention – Admit it or not, attention is sometimes only partly given to children. This is because most parents are busy with chores and other pressing matters and errands. Giving your undivided attention to your toddler is perhaps the greatest reward you will ever give them. Sadly, this does not happen all the time.

If you find it hard to do so, make sure you make up for the lost time. Make your children your priority above all other things. Yes, there may be immediate concerns to attend to, but you must find ways to do both without compromising your time and attention with them. Remember, they rely on you and you alone, so give them what is most needed.

3. Focus on what really matters – simply put, do not get drawn with the idea of having a bad day because a child misbehaves. Avoid complaining about irrelevant stuff or get so stirred up with how your child behaves. Most of all, do not ever compare your toddler to other toddlers. The trick here is to focus on what matters even if it is hard to do so. Did you know that selective deafness works sometimes? When your child shouts, "I love you, Dad", reply with "I love You too, son". But when he shouts "I hate you, Daddy!", do not get so stirred up that you will shout "I hate you, too!" back. When you are at the edge of losing your patience, know that it will get you nowhere if you will just get mad. The effects of saying such things to a child could have serious long term implications so always remember the bigger picture.

4. Stop looking for logic – because chances are, you won't find any. There is no point in saying your child exists to annoy you for the rest of your life or ruin your once serene life. Why? Because your toddler does not know what they are doing and is definitely not doing

anything of the sort. Your toddler is just being a toddler. That is it. They have a very short attention span and punishing him for disobeying you or locking him in his room will not solve the issue. A logical debate with them is a waste of time. Leave it until they come of age.

5. There must be clear communication – Positive and confident parenting is most effective if you know how to communicate well with your child. Be firm with your rules and let him know when you are upset or about to get upset. Teach him that when mommy says it is time to pick up your mess, now is the time and it must be done. But of course, you do not expect them to obey at once. If this happens, say something like, "Honey, I'll give you a hand In picking those toys. Let's both pick those up and put them in the toy box. Help me, okay?" If you start doing things like this. It is a win/win for both of you. They get to spend time with you and you help achieve the task. Start thinking in win/wins

6. Divert their attention – this is considered one of the most effective ways to disciplining toddlers. We all know that they are easily diverted. So when your toddler is about to touch an electric cord or that fancy dress of yours,

you can try diverting his attention by saying something like this "Hey, look birds!" Or, "Oh, there are dogs outside, let's go have a look." This often works. You may be lying there for a second, but this could save everybody including your sanity.

Chapter 3 – Behavior Modification Theory

Encouraging The Good, Discouraging The Bad

This is simple. Any behavior that is reinforced by rewards will tend to be repeated. So apart from using voice tones and discipline techniques, you also reward a repeat and positive performance.

Behavior modification also has a reverse side stating that any good behavior that goes unnoticed or unacknowledged will only disappear in the process. Children need to be reassured all the time. They need constant encouragement to know that they are doing well. In toddlers, behavior modification will work best if the good behavior gets to be rewarded in an instant. This technique must be used consistently in order for it to become effective. On the other hand, if bad behavior is going to be ignored and underplayed just so your child knows that he has no audience to impress, you may allow four to five occurrences before doing something about the behavior.

The Rewards

Rewarding toddlers for a job well done regardless if it is about behaving well in public places or getting along well with other kids should be performed because that is just how things are. Put it this way, you get rewarded with money for working, you get extra pay for extra work, or your older kids get good grades for studying hard. Simply put, if rewarding adults is thought appropriate, why not children, right?

The Soft Rewards

These refer to rewards that primarily makes use of attention, smile, touch, praises, hugs and kisses. When used wisely and cautiously, this can be all powerful and effective. When misused, it could promote undesirable behaviors. Toddlers are sensitive to this kind of reward, and they often give in to these simply because they love being praised, cuddled, and noticed by their parents given their age.

The Hard Rewards

These can be in the form of items such as a star stamp, smiley sticker, or a "good job" chart. These work for children who are in their preschool. You may also want to give them sweet treats and other kiddie stuff.

Soft or Hard Rewards? Which one is best?

When deciding whether to go for soft or hard rewards, your child's age is an important factor to consider. Toddlers are more content with soft rewards while older toddlers are more enticed with the idea of having stickers or sweets if they behaved well. Just remember that the very purpose of behavior modification is to reward a good behavior that has happened. You shouldn't do this by offering them the reward beforehand as eventually they will start asking or expecting an incentive before they do anything. This technique will help you steer a challenging and stubborn toddler around without ruining your already demanding day.

Another common example of behavior modification is when it comes to feeding. Toddlers are picky eaters or would rather not eat at all. As with this behavior modification, what a parent like you must do is put the food in front of your toddler. He either picks up or eats the food, or he ends up hungry and asks for a bottle of milk. You do not insist, do airplane noises, juggles fruits, or scold at your child. You just let him decide what he is going to do with the food. If he eats, then good for the both of you. But when he rejects, just ignore. There is a higher chance that he will end up eating the food. Now, that is maintained sanity and no future fights over food. Also, children can start to relate eating with stress which can lead to all types of problems so meal time should not be a big deal to them.

Changes will come little y little

You do not devise a behavior plan and apply it to your child all convinced that it will work only after hours of doing it. Behavior modifications would take time and practice. There is no point expecting a child to instantly transform himself from being untamed to a refined one. You have to allow weeks and months to see the real change.

As you utilize behavior modifications, you have to remember to keep your defenses strong and show that there is a new you who is in charge and means business. Sometimes, you even have to put up with a bit of extra pain in order to reap long-term rewards. If you are dedicated to making this technique work for your child, you have to be prepared to handle and go through dark and difficult times before you finally see results, good results.

Smacking just won't cut it

Smacking or using force against a child as a form of discipline is wrong. While there are those who resort to occasional smack, there are also those who frequently beat their children. Remember, this will set a bad example to children and will remember unhappy experiences when they grow up. Children also learn from you if you resort to violence when you can't solve a problem, it is likely that they will start to think the same

Chapter 4 – Dealing with Toddler Tantrums

Now with all the theories and techniques laid before you from the previous chapters, now is the time to put all of them in practice. How do you stay composed as your toddler starts to scream and cry louder and louder? How do you deal with a child who refuses to hear your commands? And what about those regular tantrums?

Tantrums are a toddler's trademark. They start at around their first year until such time that they are able to find ways to get what they want when they want it. While children are born different, some you can easily control, there are others with a short fuse. Disciplining them would mean expecting that there will be a mess all around.

In a toddler's eyes, a tantrum can be brought about by many different stimuli. This can be from inner frustrations or him being impatient of himself and others. To treat tantrums, it would rely greatly on the age your toddler is in. From ages 1 to 2 1/2 years, your toddler's behavior can be soothed with gentleness and a good dose of understanding. At the age of 3, a child uses a tantrum to resist his parents' orders. This is where you should be consistent and firm enough in your rules. Let this point be clear to him that there is no way he can get things his way and throwing a tantrum is not just worth the effort.

Tantrums – The Major Battle

Every day, you are confronted with many different kinds of tantrums. On center stage is a child who is being prevented from doing something that will either endanger him or the things around him. Notice that first, he takes a good look at his surroundings in preparation for one spectacular show. Next, he takes a look at his audience and their reactions. And then finally, in just a flash, he does it and the performance of his lifetime is on.

Tackling tantrums may not be an easy one, but they can be dealt with. Take a look at the following examples and see how you can handle tantrums of different kinds:

There are ideal methods for handling tantrums based on the reason for the tantrum in the first place

This is where you need to assess the situation and your surroundings to decide why is the tantrum happening in the first place. Once you know the reason for the tantrum you can take the appropriate response. Here are the main three reasons tantrums happen and the guidelines for dealing with each one:

1. The child wants your attention. If the Child is throwing a tantrum for your attention, pay them no attention whatsoever. If you can, leave the room, you will thus be removing their audience and showing them it is not an effective way to get what they want. You'll find that this might cause them to up their antics in a desperate case to win your attention back. However, they will not continue this too long once they realize it isn't working. it might take a couple of goes but stick to it. If you give in once they'll see a chink in your armor so you have to stick to your guns on it.

2. If the tantrum is because of your child's inability to communicate what they want or if it's because of their inability to do something that's causing them to be

frustrated then: Firmly explain that their behavior is not ok and then to figure out a way to encourage them and help them. Teach them that if they are patient and they don't give up, they can succeed. This will also help them to develop this quality that will carry through with them for the rest of their life.

3. If a child is being deliberately destructive or is in danger of harming others; a time out is in order. Take your child and place them in their room or in a safe space alone. Sometimes children struggle to calm down on their own, however. Activities such as singing a song or an activity might help.

On tidying up toys

While some children seem to be born organized and tidy, the majority are quite messy, and they love being like that. The former can be easily trained, while the latter would be a bit challenging. To make things easier for parents like you, you can try the following tips:

- Try restricting the number of toys your toddler has.

- Allot a big box for toys and make it a habit to let your child clear up his toys and put them in the box after playing.

Tidy up with your child and have it be a fun time for both of you.

- Make tidy not just a habit but also a form of play. The moment you say the word "Tidy", have your toddler pick whatever toy lying on the floor and put it inside the box. Make this fun and exciting for your little one.

Change Their Emotions Not Their Mind

Toddlers have not yet developed the ability to use logic and reason. There is no point trying to win on this front. Instead, try changing the circumstances completely. The scenarios that lead to a child getting angry or throwing tantrums can often be changed. When you change the way the child perceives an event, the event itself changes. Try to flip the script on the child, if they hate meal times, try to think of a way you could add something in, that's enjoyable for both of you. Maybe you devote some attention to them. You could have a race to see who could tidy up the fastest.

When you start getting angry, the child cannot always understand why. Often toddlers can be like quicksand; the more you struggle, the quicker you sink. You can try shouting and using force all you want. Instead, sometimes it's best to go the opposite way and be almost devoid of emotion on the topic at hand. If they get next to zero emotional response from you, it is not satisfying for them. You can reward them when they do good, however when they do bad, be firm and tell them, but try to take emotion out of it. Your child's emotions are their main driving force if you learn to guide their emotional state you will learn to guide them.

Build a rapport with the child

A rapport is building a relationship with the child where it's clear you understand each other's feelings and concerns. If the child is upset try, understand where they are coming from. If the child can sense you have built a rapport with them, they are more likely to feel the concerns understood and less likely to act out. It is how you are making them feel that matters, not trying to outsmart them with logic, they don't speak that language yet. This helps you better understand your child. If your toddler refuses to share their toy, trying going down to their level(this helps in building rapport) and asking them about it. Sometimes a child just needs to experience owning something before they are ready to give it away. You want to instill the belief that this is ok and that it would be great if they did share, it would make you really happy but ultimately they have a choice. This will teach your child to do things like sharing because they want to and not because they have to.

How to build a rapport with a child

To try and build a rapport with the child: firstly as stated before, get down to their level and try to feel what they're feeling and empathize with them. An example in the adult world of this is: If two people meet and one of them starts telling them of something bad that happened them, it would be strange if the second person didn't meet their emotional state. Imagine you were telling them something that really hurt you, and they stood there smiling, you wouldn't feel very understood. So try putting yourself in your child's shoes and feeling what they're feeling when you are listening to them.

Use positive instead of negative language

It is a human quality to want to do something when we are told we can't. Instead of asking your child to stop messing around, ask them could they stand still. Instead of saying don't touch that, ask them can they keep their hands by their side. When we tell them they can't do something, it creates this irresistible urge a lot of the time to do the very thing we're telling them not to. The same psychological drivers that exist in us as adults exists in children.

Conclusion

Thank you again for downloading this book!

I hope this book was able to help you deal with difficult and challenging toddlers. Whether your toddler is active or explosive, or both, these children somehow put immense strain on you as a parent. But that should not be the end of the world for you. The techniques that you have learned from this book will help you on your journey towards taming your child and eventually raise a kid that is well-mannered and well-behaved.

The next step is to try all these tips and techniques. Know what works for you and your toddler best. Remember, every day is a new learning experience. You may have challenging days and have somehow lost on those days, but know that you can rise up again and win over your flaws.

Parenting is a beautiful journey; something that you will take on for many years and yet will still miss especially when your children come of age and step out of the house. So be grateful that you still have time to nurture and be with them. You will surely miss those tantrums, diaper change, and all about this messy yet rewarding job called parenting.

Finally, if you enjoyed this book, then I'd like to ask you for a favor, would you be kind enough to leave a review for this book on Amazon? It'd be greatly appreciated!

Thank you and good luck!

Printed in Great Britain
by Amazon